PRAISE FOR **k** ⌐⌐⌐⌐⌐

MW01493353

From *"The Power of Impact Investing:"*

The Power of Impact Investing guidebook is a great resource for anyone interested in making a positive impact with their investments. It's easy to understand especially for a newbie like me, and it covers a wide range of topics, including social entrepreneurship, sustainable development goals, and corporate social responsibility. The book is packed with useful strategies and advice on how to invest in businesses and projects that create social and environmental benefits, while still also earning financial returns. Whether you're a seasoned investor or just starting out like me, this guidebook is sure to help you make a difference in the world while you try to grow on your own.

— CHELSEA AN

I've been looking to invest in sustainable environmental sources but needed help finding them. This book broke down the different types of social and ecological investments while also talking about their ups and down of them—such a valuable book to have on hand when making decisions.

— MAGEN HAYASHI

"Great Information, Even Better Presentation."

— BROOKE

THE POWER OF IMPACT INVESTING

THE POWER OF IMPACT INVESTING

A GUIDEBOOK FOR STRATEGIES, SECTORS,
SUSTAINABLE DEVELOPMENT GOALS, SOCIAL
ENTREPRENEURSHIP, CORPORATE SOCIAL
RESPONSIBILITY, AND MORE

SOCIALLY RESPONSIBLE INVESTING

ROBERT BUCKLEY

BOOK BOUND STUDIOS

To my family for their unwavering support and encouragement throughout the writing of this book. And to my mentor and friend Justina, whose guidance and wisdom have been invaluable in shaping my understanding of impact investing.

The greatest threat to our planet is the belief that someone else will save it.

— ROBERT SWAN

CONTENTS

$10.99 FREE EBOOK

Receive Your Free Copy of The Power of Intelligent Investing

Or visit:
bookboundstudios.wixsite.com/robert-buckley

INTRODUCTION

Impact investing is a powerful tool that can help create positive social and environmental change while generating financial returns. This chapter will explore the definition, history, importance, types, and key players of impact investing.

Definition of Impact Investing

Impact investing is a relatively new concept that has gained significant traction recently. It is a form of investment that goes beyond the traditional focus on financial returns and instead prioritizes **social and environmental impact**. The goal of impact investing is to create positive change in the world while still earning a profit.

The concept of impact investing is rooted in the belief that businesses are responsible for contributing to society and the environment. Therefore, impact investors seek out companies committed to positively impacting and willing to support them financially. This can take many forms, from investing in renewable energy projects to funding education initiatives in underserved communities.

One of the key features of impact investing is the emphasis on measuring and reporting on social and environmental outcomes. Impact investors want to see tangible evidence that their investments are making a difference, and they use a variety of metrics to track progress. This includes everything from carbon emissions reductions to improvements in health outcomes for disadvantaged populations.

Impact investing is not just for wealthy individuals or institutional investors. There are now a growing number of impact investment funds and platforms that allow everyday investors to participate. This democratization of impact investing can drive even greater positive change as more people become aware of the power of their investments to make a difference.

Overall, impact investing is a powerful tool for creating positive change in the world. By aligning financial goals with social and environmental objectives, impact investors can help address some of society's most pressing challenges. Whether you are an individual investor or a large institution, there are many opportunities to get involved in impact investing and make a difference.

History of Impact Investing

The concept of impact investing has been around for decades, tracing back to the 1960s. During this time, socially responsible investing emerged as a way for individuals to align their investments with personal values. This approach was driven by a desire to invest in companies that positively impacted society, such as being environmentally friendly or promoting social justice.

However, it was in the 1980s that the idea of impact investing began to take shape. This was when microfinance institutions started to provide small loans to low-income individuals and entrepreneurs in developing countries. These loans were designed to help people start or grow their businesses. They quickly became a powerful tool for poverty reduction.

As the microfinance industry grew, so too did the idea of **impact investing**. Investors began to see the potential for using their money to impact society while positively generating financial returns. This led to the development of the impact investing industry in the 2000s, which has since become a major force in finance.

Today, impact investing is a rapidly growing field encompassing many investment strategies and approaches. From investing in renewable energy projects to supporting social enterprises, impact investors use their money to drive positive change in the world. And as the world faces increasingly complex social and environmental challenges, the importance of impact investing is only set to grow.

Importance of Impact Investing

Impact investing is a crucial tool in the fight against social and environmental challenges that have plagued our world for decades. It is a powerful means of mobilizing private capital to address issues that governments and philanthropy alone cannot solve. By investing in companies and organizations that prioritize social and environmental impact, impact investors can help create a more sustainable and equitable future for all.

One of the most significant benefits of impact investing is its ability to generate financial returns for investors while simultaneously **creating positive social and environmental outcomes**. This is achieved by investing in companies committed to making a difference in the world through sustainable business practices, social entrepreneurship, or innovative solutions to pressing global issues.

Moreover, impact investing can help create new markets, products, and services that benefit society and the environment. By investing in companies developing new technologies or business models that prioritize sustainability and social impact, impact investors can help drive innovation and progress in these areas.

Another key advantage of impact investing is its potential to drive **systemic change**. By investing in companies and organizations that are working to address systemic issues such as poverty, inequality, and climate change, impact investors can help create a more just and sustainable world. Businesses can achieve this by supporting social and environmental justice initiatives, such as community development projects, renewable energy initiatives, and sustainable agriculture programs.

In conclusion, impact investing is critical for creating positive social and environmental outcomes while generating financial returns for investors. In addition, by investing in companies and organizations that prioritize sustainability and social impact, impact investors can help drive innovation, create new markets, and promote systemic change. As such, impact investing is essential to any strategy to create a more just and sustainable future for all.

Types of Impact Investing

Impact investing is a rapidly growing field that has gained significant traction recently. It is a form of investing that seeks to generate positive social and environmental outcomes alongside financial returns. There are several types of impact investing, each with unique characteristics, risks, and opportunities.

One of the most popular forms of impact investing is **social impact bonds**. These financial instruments allow investors to fund social programs and initiatives that address specific social issues, such as homelessness, education, or healthcare. Social impact bonds are structured, so investors receive a return on their investment only if the program achieves its predetermined social outcomes.

Another type of impact investing is **green bonds**. These fixed-income securities fund environmentally friendly projects, such as renewable energy, energy efficiency, or sustainable agriculture. Green bonds are becoming increasingly popular as investors seek to align their investments with their values and support the transition to a low-carbon economy.

Community investing is another form of impact investing focusing on providing capital to underserved communities and businesses. This type of investing aims to promote economic development and social equity by supporting small businesses, affordable housing, and community facilities in low-income areas.

Microfinance is another type of impact investing that provides financial services, such as loans, savings, and insurance, to low-income individuals and communities. Microfinance institutions aim to promote financial inclusion and empower individuals to improve their livelihoods and break the cycle of poverty.

Finally, **venture philanthropy** is a form of impact investing that combines the principles of venture capital with philanthropy. Venture philanthropists invest in social enterprises and nonprofits that have the potential to generate significant social impact and financial returns. They provide financial, strategic, and operational support to help these organizations achieve their goals.

In conclusion, impact investing offers a range of opportunities for investors to generate positive social and environmental outcomes alongside financial returns. By understanding the different types of impact investing and their unique characteristics, investors can choose the approach that best aligns with their values and investment goals.

Key Players in Impact Investing

The world of impact investing is a complex and multifaceted ecosystem comprising a diverse range of key players. These players include impact investors, social entrepreneurs, philanthropists, foundations, development finance institutions, and governments. Each of these players has a unique role in advancing the field of impact investing and achieving positive social and environmental outcomes.

Impact investors are individuals or organizations that invest in companies or projects to generate a measurable social or environmental impact alongside a financial return. They are often motivated by a desire to create positive change in the world and to use their capital to address pressing social and environmental challenges.

Social entrepreneurs, on the other hand, are individuals or organizations that use business models to create social or environmental impact. They are often driven by a desire to solve a specific social or environmental problem and to create sustainable solutions that can be scaled and replicated.

Philanthropists and foundations also play a critical role in impact investing. They provide funding and support to social entrepreneurs and impact investors, often focusing on specific issues such as education, healthcare, or the environment. They also help to build the infrastructure and networks needed to support the growth of the impact investing field.

Development finance institutions, such as the World Bank or the International Finance Corporation, are specialized organizations that provide financing and technical assistance to support economic development in developing countries. They often work closely with impact investors and social entrepreneurs to help them access the capital and resources they need to scale their impact.

Finally, **governments** also have an important role to play in impact investing. They can create policies and regulations that support the growth of the impact investing field, such as tax incentives or impact reporting requirements. They can also provide funding and support for social entrepreneurs and impact investors, particularly in areas where the private sector may be hesitant to invest.

In summary, the impact investing ecosystem comprises diverse key players, each with a unique role in advancing the field and achieving positive social and environmental outcomes. These players can help create a more just and sustainable world by working together.

In conclusion, impact investing is a powerful tool that can help create positive social and environmental change while generating financial returns. By understanding the definition, history, importance, types, and key players of impact investing, we can become more informed and engaged investors who can make a difference in the world.

1

UNDERSTANDING IMPACT INVESTING

A tree growing out of a piggy bank, symbolizing the positive impact of investing in sustainable agriculture.

I mpact investing is a rapidly growing field that seeks to create positive social and environmental outcomes while generating financial returns. It is a powerful tool for investors who want to align their investments with their values and make a difference in the world. In this chapter, we will explore the principles of impact investing, the importance of impact measurement and evaluation, the risks and challenges of impact investing, how it differs from traditional investing, and the unique opportunities and challenges of impact investing in developing countries.

Principles of Impact Investing

Impact investing is a unique approach to investing that is guided by a set of principles that distinguish it from traditional investing. These principles are intentionality, additionality, measurability, and accountability. Let's take a closer look at each of these principles.

Intentionality is a key principle of impact investing. It means that investors seek to create positive social and environmental outcomes alongside financial returns. In other words, impact investors focus on making money rather than positively impacting the world. This is a fundamental difference between impact investing and traditional investing.

Another important principle of impact investing is **additionality**. This means that impact investments should not displace existing funding sources but instead provide new capital to address unmet needs. Impact investors are looking to fill gaps in the market and provide funding to projects that might not otherwise receive it.

Measurability is also a critical principle of impact investing. Investors should track and report on their investments' social and environmental outcomes. This is important because it allows investors to see the impact of their investments and make adjustments as needed. Measuring impact is not always easy, but ensuring that investments make a positive difference is essential.

Finally, **accountability** is a key principle of impact investing.

Investors should be transparent about their impact and accountable to their stakeholders. This means that impact investors should be open about their investments and the impact they are having. They should also be accountable to the communities they are investing in and ensure that their investments align with the needs and priorities of those communities.

To be effective, impact investors must also consider the context in which they invest. This means understanding the social, economic, and environmental factors affecting the communities they invest in. It also means engaging with stakeholders, including the communities, to ensure that investments align with their needs and priorities. Finally, impact investors must be aware of their investments' impact and be willing to make changes if necessary.

In conclusion, impact investing is a unique approach to investing that is guided by a set of principles that distinguish it from traditional investing. These principles include intentionality, additionality, measurability, and accountability. To be effective, impact investors must also consider the context in which they invest and engage with stakeholders to ensure that their investments align with the needs and priorities of the communities they are investing in.

Impact Measurement and Evaluation

In today's world, investing is **not just about financial returns.** Investors are increasingly looking for ways to impact society and the environment positively. Impact investing is a growing trend seeking to generate financial returns and positive social and environmental outcomes. However, measuring and evaluating the impact of these investments is critical to their success.

Impact measurement and evaluation allow investors to understand their investments' social and environmental outcomes. As a result, it helps them make informed decisions about future investments and ensures that their investments are making a positive impact. However, measuring impact can be challenging, as social and environmental outcomes are often difficult to quantify and measure.

To address this challenge, impact investors use various tools and frameworks. One such tool is the **Impact Management Project**, which provides a standardized approach to measuring and managing impact. It helps investors define and measure impact, set targets and benchmarks, and report on their progress.

Another tool is the **Global Impact Investing Network's Impact Reporting and Investment Standards**. This framework provides guidelines for impact investors to report on their investments' social and environmental outcomes. It helps investors communicate their impact to stakeholders and ensures transparency and accountability.

Finally, the **United Nations Sustainable Development Goals** provide a framework for investors to align their investments with global sustainability goals. The SDGs provide a set of 17 goals and 169 targets that address social, economic, and environmental issues. By aligning their investments with these goals, investors can ensure they positively impact society and the environment.

In conclusion, measuring and evaluating the impact of investments is critical to the success of impact investing. Impact investors use various tools and frameworks to address the challenge of measuring impact, including the Impact Management Project, the Global Impact Investing Network's Impact Reporting and Investment Standards, and the United Nations Sustainable Development Goals. Using these tools, investors can ensure that their investments positively impact society and the environment.

Risks and Challenges of Impact Investing

Impact investing is a unique strategy to generate positive social and environmental outcomes and financial returns. However, like any investment, it carries risks that must be carefully considered and managed. These risks can be broadly categorized into financial, social, and environmental.

Financial risks are the most obvious risks associated with impact investing. As with any investment, there is always the possibility of losing money. Therefore, impact investors must carefully evaluate the financial viability of their investments and ensure that they are making sound financial decisions. This requires a thorough understanding of the market, the investment opportunity, and the potential risks and rewards.

In addition to financial risks, impact investors must consider **social and environmental risks.** These risks can arise when the intended positive impact of an investment is not realized or when unintended negative consequences occur. For example, investing in a renewable energy project may have unintended negative consequences for local communities if it displaces people from their homes or disrupts traditional livelihoods.

To mitigate these risks, impact investors must conduct thorough due diligence before making investment decisions. This involves researching the investment opportunity, assessing the potential risks and rewards, and engaging with stakeholders to understand their perspectives and concerns. Impact investors must also be willing to adapt their strategies as needed to ensure they achieve their intended social and environmental outcomes.

Working in complex social and environmental contexts can also present challenges for impact investors. For example, addressing systemic issues like poverty and climate change requires a long-term, collaborative approach that involves multiple stakeholders. Impact investors must be able to navigate these complex contexts and build strong partnerships with other investors, governments, and civil society organizations.

In conclusion, impact investing carries risks that must be carefully considered and managed. However, impact investors can mitigate these risks by conducting thorough due diligence, engaging with stakeholders, building strong partnerships, and achieving their intended social and environmental outcomes. Ultimately, impact investing has the potential to generate positive change in the world while also generating financial returns for investors.

Impact Investing vs. Traditional Investing

When it comes to investing, there are two main approaches: **traditional investing** and **impact investing.** While both aim to generate returns on investment, their priorities and methods differ.

Traditional investing is primarily focused on financial returns. Investors seek to maximize profits by investing in companies and assets expected to perform well in the short term. This approach often relies on financial metrics, such as return on investment, to measure success.

In contrast, impact investing seeks to create positive social and environmental outcomes alongside financial returns. This means that impact investors prioritize investments that positively impact society and the environment and generate financial returns. In addition, impact investing takes a longer-term view, recognizing that social and environmental change often requires sustained effort over time.

While traditional and impact investing may seem like opposing approaches, they are not mutually exclusive. For example, many impact investors use traditional investment strategies, such as diversification and risk management, alongside impact-focused strategies. This allows them to generate financial returns while also making a positive impact on society and the environment.

One of the key differences between traditional and impact investing is the metrics used to measure success. Traditional investing tends to focus on financial metrics, such as return on investment and earnings per share. Impact investing, on the other hand, uses broader metrics, including social and environmental impact. This means that impact investors may prioritize investments that positively impact issues such as climate change, poverty, and inequality, even if they may not generate the highest financial returns in the short term.

Overall, impact investing represents a shift in how we think about investing. It recognizes that financial returns are not the only measure of success and that investors are responsible for considering their investments' impact on society and the environment. While impact investing is still a relatively new approach, it has the potential to drive positive change and create a more sustainable and equitable future.

Impact Investing in Developing Countries

Impact investing in developing countries is a complex and multifaceted endeavor that requires a deep understanding of these countries' unique opportunities and challenges. On the one hand, developing countries often face significant social and environmental challenges that impact investors can help address. These challenges may include poverty, lack of access to basic services such as healthcare and education, and environmental degradation.

However, investing in developing countries also comes with its own set of challenges. These countries often have complex political and economic contexts that make investing challenging. For example, corruption, weak governance, and unstable economies can all pose significant risks to investors.

To be effective in developing countries, impact investors must be willing to put in the time and effort to **understand the local context**. This means engaging with local stakeholders, including community members, government officials, and civil society organizations. By building strong partnerships with local organizations, impact investors can better understand the needs and priorities of the communities they are working with.

In addition, impact investors must be willing to take a long-term view and be patient in achieving their impact goals. Creating sustainable change in developing countries often takes time and requires a deep commitment to the communities being served. Therefore, impact investors must be willing to invest in projects and initiatives that may yield little results but that have the potential to create lasting change over time.

Ultimately, impact investing in developing countries is a powerful tool for creating positive social and environmental change. By understanding the unique opportunities and challenges these countries present, impact investors can make a meaningful difference in the lives of millions of people worldwide.

Impact investing is a powerful tool for investors who want to create positive social and environmental outcomes while generating financial returns. However, to be effective, impact investors must be guided by a set of principles that distinguish them from traditional investing, measure and evaluate their impact, navigate risks and challenges, understand the differences between impact investing and traditional investing, and be willing to adapt their strategies to the unique opportunities and challenges of investing in developing countries.

Chapter Summary

- Impact investing is guided by principles that distinguish it from traditional investing.
- Measuring and evaluating impact is critical to the success of impact investing.
- Impact investing carries financial, social, and environmental risks.
- Impact investing differs from traditional investing in its focus on social and environmental outcomes.
- Impact investing in developing countries presents unique opportunities and challenges.
- Impact investors must understand the local context and engage with local stakeholders.
- Impact investors must take a long-term view and be patient in achieving their impact goals.
- Impact investing and traditional investing are not mutually exclusive.

2

IMPACT INVESTING STRATEGIES

A tree with roots deeply entrenched in the earth, symbolizing the long-term impact of sustainable investing strategies.

I mpact investing is a growing trend in the investment world. Investors seek to positively impact society and the environment while earning a financial return. Impact investing strategies are diverse, ranging from socially responsible investing to microfinance. This chapter will explore five impact investing strategies that are gaining popularity: socially responsible investing, environmental, social, and governance (ESG) investing, community investing, microfinance, and impact bonds. We will discuss the benefits and challenges of each strategy and provide examples of successful impact investments.

Socially Responsible Investing

Socially responsible investing (SRI) is an investment strategy considering financial return and social and environmental impact. SRI investors seek to invest in companies that align with their values and avoid companies that engage in harmful practices. Investors can achieve SRI through negative screening, positive screening, or shareholder advocacy. Negative screening involves excluding companies that engage in activities such as tobacco, weapons, or fossil fuels. Positive screening involves investing in companies that positively impact society and the environment, such as renewable energy or sustainable agriculture. Finally, shareholder advocacy involves using shareholder power to influence corporate behavior.

SRI has gained popularity recently, with more investors seeking to align their investments with their values. SRI funds have also performed well, with some outperforming traditional funds. However, SRI has challenges, such as defining socially responsible behavior and balancing financial return with social and environmental impact. Despite these challenges, SRI is a powerful tool for investors to impact society and the environment positively.

Environmental, Social, and Governance (ESG) Investing

ESG investing is an investment strategy that considers environmental, social, and governance factors in addition to financial return. ESG investors seek to invest in companies that positively impact society and the environment and are well-governed. ESG factors include climate change, human rights, labor standards, board diversity, and executive compensation. ESG investing can be achieved through integration, engagement, or impact investing. Integration involves incorporating ESG factors into traditional investment analysis. Engagement involves using shareholder power to influence corporate behavior. Impact investing involves investing in companies or projects with a specific social or environmental impact.

ESG investing has gained popularity in recent years, with more investors recognizing the importance of considering non-financial factors in investment decisions. ESG funds have also performed well, with some outperforming traditional funds. However, ESG has its challenges, such as defining ESG factors and measuring their impact. Despite these challenges, ESG is a powerful tool for investors to impact society and the environment positively.

Suppose you're interested in learning more about ESG investing. In that case, you can find my other book, *"The Power of ESG Investing,"* at your favorite book retailer.

Community Investing

Community investing is an investment strategy that seeks to provide capital to underserved communities and support community development. Community investors invest in community development financial institutions (CDFIs) or other organizations that provide loans or other financial services to low-income communities. Community investing can support affordable housing, small business development, and job creation in underserved communities.

Community investing has a long history in the United States, with CDFIs providing critical support to low-income communities. Community investing has also gained popularity recently, with more investors recognizing the importance of supporting underserved communities. However, community investing has challenges, such as finding viable investment opportunities in underserved communities and balancing financial return with social impact. Despite these challenges, community investing is a powerful tool for investors to support community development and promote economic justice.

Microfinance

Microfinance is an investment strategy that provides small loans and other financial services to low-income individuals and small businesses in developing countries. Microfinance can support entrepreneurship, job creation, and poverty reduction in developing countries. Microfinance institutions (MFIs) provide loans, savings accounts, and other financial services to low-income individuals and small businesses.

Microfinance has gained popularity recently, with more investors recognizing the importance of supporting entrepreneurship and economic development in developing countries. Microfinance has also been successful in promoting financial inclusion and poverty reduction. However, microfinance has challenges, such as finding viable investment opportunities in developing countries and balancing financial return with social impact. Despite these challenges, microfinance is a powerful tool for investors to support economic development and promote financial inclusion in developing countries.

Impact Bonds

Impact bonds are a financing mechanism that provides funding for social or environmental programs based on their outcomes. Impact bonds involve a partnership between investors, service providers, and government agencies. Investors fund social or environmental programs, and service providers deliver the programs. If the programs achieve their desired outcomes, the government agency pays the investors a return.

Impact bonds have gained popularity in recent years, with more investors recognizing the importance of measuring social and environmental impact. Impact bonds have also successfully promoted innovation and collaboration in social and environmental programs. However, impact bonds have challenges, such as defining outcomes and measuring impact. Despite these challenges, impact bonds are a powerful tool for investors to support social and environmental programs and promote innovation and collaboration.

Impact investing strategies are diverse and powerful tools for investors to impact society and the environment positively. Each strategy has its benefits and challenges, but all can provide financial returns and social and environmental impact. By considering impact investing strategies, investors can align their investments with their values and support positive social and environmental change.

Chapter Summary

- Socially responsible investing considers financial return and social and environmental impact.
- Environmental, social, and governance (ESG) investing considers ESG factors in addition to financial return.
- Community investing provides capital to underserved communities and supports community development.
- Microfinance provides small loans and other financial services to low-income individuals and small businesses in developing countries.
- Impact bonds fund social or environmental programs based on their outcomes.
- SRI, ESG, community investing, microfinance, and impact bonds are powerful tools for investors to positively impact society and the environment.
- Impact investing strategies have benefits and challenges, but all can provide financial return and social and environmental impact.
- By considering impact investing strategies, investors can align their investments with their values and support positive social and environmental change.

3

IMPACT INVESTING SECTORS

A city skyline at night, with green energy solutions like wind turbines and solar panels prominently featured on rooftops.

I mpact investing is a rapidly growing field that aims to generate positive social and environmental impact alongside financial returns. Impact investors seek to invest in companies and organizations making a difference worldwide. Several sectors are particularly popular for impact investing. This chapter will explore five sectors: education, healthcare, renewable energy, agriculture, and affordable housing. We will examine the impact investments in these sectors can have and highlight some of the most promising opportunities for impact investors.

Education

Investing in education is one of the most impactful ways to create positive change in the world. Education is the key to unlocking human potential and is essential for economic growth and social development. Impact investors can invest in various education-related initiatives, including schools, training programs, and educational technology companies.

Investments in education can have a wide range of positive impacts. For example, investing in schools can help to improve access to education for children in underserved communities. Investing in training programs can equip people with the skills they need to succeed in the workforce. And investing in educational technology companies can help to create innovative solutions that make learning more engaging and effective.

There are several promising opportunities for impact investors in the education sector. One example is investing in companies that provide affordable and accessible online education. Another example is investing in schools that serve low-income communities and provide high-quality education. As a result, impact investors can help create a brighter future for individuals and communities worldwide by investing in education.

Healthcare

Investing in healthcare is another impactful way to create positive change in the world. Access to healthcare is essential for human well-being and a key driver of economic growth and social development. Impact investors can invest in various healthcare-related initiatives, including hospitals, clinics, and medical technology companies.

Investments in healthcare can have a wide range of positive impacts. For example, investing in hospitals and clinics can help improve healthcare access for people in underserved communities. Investing in medical technology companies can help to create innovative solutions that improve the quality and efficiency of healthcare. Finally, investing in healthcare training programs can equip people with the skills they need to provide high-quality care.

There are several promising opportunities for impact investors in the healthcare sector. One example is investing in companies that provide affordable and accessible healthcare services. Another example is investing in medical technology companies developing innovative solutions to healthcare challenges. By investing in healthcare, impact investors can help improve the health and well-being of individuals and communities worldwide.

Renewable Energy

Investing in renewable energy is a powerful way to create positive change in the world. Renewable energy is essential for reducing greenhouse gas emissions and mitigating the impacts of climate change. Impact investors can invest in various renewable energy initiatives, including solar, wind, and hydroelectric power projects.

Investments in renewable energy can have a wide range of positive impacts. For example, investing in solar power projects can reduce reliance on fossil fuels and decrease greenhouse gas emissions. Investing in wind power projects can create jobs and stimulate economic growth in rural communities. And investing in hydroelectric power projects can help to provide clean energy to communities that lack access to electricity.

There are several promising opportunities for impact investors in the renewable energy sector. One example is investing in companies that develop and manufacture renewable energy technologies. Another example is investing in renewable energy projects that provide affordable and accessible energy to underserved communities. By investing in renewable energy, impact investors can help to create a more sustainable and equitable future for all.

Agriculture

Investing in agriculture is a powerful way to create positive change in the world. Agriculture is essential for food security and economic development and is a key social and environmental sustainability driver. Impact investors can invest in various agriculture-related initiatives, including sustainable farming practices, food processing and distribution, and agricultural technology companies.

Investments in agriculture can have a wide range of positive impacts. For example, investing in sustainable farming practices can help to improve soil health, reduce water usage, and increase crop yields. Investing in food processing and distribution can create jobs and stimulate economic growth in rural communities. And investing in agricultural technology companies can help to create innovative solutions that improve the efficiency and sustainability of agriculture.

There are several promising opportunities for impact investors in the agriculture sector. One example is investing in companies that develop and manufacture sustainable farming technologies. Another example is investing in food processing and distribution companies that prioritize social and environmental sustainability. By investing in agriculture, impact investors can help to create a more sustainable and equitable food system for all.

Affordable Housing

Investing in affordable housing is a powerful way to create positive change in the world. Access to safe and affordable housing is essential for human well-being and a key driver of economic growth and social development. Impact investors can invest in various affordable housing initiatives, including housing developments, community land trusts, and housing cooperatives.

Investments in affordable housing can have a wide range of positive impacts. For example, investing in affordable housing can help provide safe and stable housing for low-income families. Investing in community land trusts can help to create affordable housing that is permanently affordable and community-controlled. And investing in housing cooperatives can help to create a sense of community and shared ownership among residents.

There are several promising opportunities for impact investors in the affordable housing sector. One example is investing in affordable housing developments prioritizing social and environmental sustainability. Another example is investing in community land trusts prioritizing community control and resident participation. By investing in affordable housing, impact investors can help to create a more equitable and sustainable housing system for all.

Impact investing in education, healthcare, renewable energy, agriculture, and affordable housing can have a powerful and positive impact on individuals and communities worldwide. By investing in these sectors, impact investors can help to create a more sustainable, equitable, and prosperous future for all.

Chapter Summary

- Investing in education can improve access to education, training, and educational technology.
- Investing in healthcare can improve access to healthcare, medical technology, and training.
- Investing in renewable energy can reduce greenhouse gas emissions and provide clean energy to underserved communities.

- Investing in agriculture can improve soil health, increase crop yields, and create sustainable food systems.
- Investing in affordable housing can provide safe and stable housing for low-income families and create community-controlled housing.
- Promising opportunities for impact investors in education include affordable and accessible online education and schools that serve low-income communities.
- Promising opportunities for impact investors in healthcare include affordable and accessible healthcare services and medical technology companies that develop innovative solutions to healthcare challenges.
- Promising opportunities for impact investors in renewable energy, agriculture, and affordable housing include investing in sustainable technologies, community-controlled initiatives, and projects prioritizing social and environmental sustainability.

4

IMPACT INVESTING IN ACTION

A plant growing in a desert, symbolizing the transformative power of impact investing to turn seemingly barren or hopeless situations into thriving and sustainable communities.

I mpact investing is a powerful tool to drive social and environmental change while generating financial returns. This chapter will explore the impact investing landscape and showcase successful case studies from the public and private sectors, philanthropy, and the nonprofit sector. We will also examine each sector's unique challenges and opportunities in implementing impact investing strategies. By the end of this chapter, you will have a deeper understanding of how impact investing can create positive change and how you can get involved.

Case Studies of Successful Impact Investments

Impact investing has the potential to create significant social and environmental impact while generating financial returns. In this section, we will explore some successful case studies that demonstrate the power of impact investing. One such example is the Acumen Fund, which invests in companies that provide essential goods and services to low-income communities in developing countries. Through its investments, Acumen has helped to improve millions of people's access to healthcare, education, and clean energy.

Another successful impact investment is the Social Investment Business, which provides loans and grants to social enterprises in the UK. Since its inception, the Social Investment Business has invested over £450 million in more than 3,500 social enterprises (Social Investment Business, 2022), creating jobs and improving the lives of people in local communities.

Individuals can also use impact investing to address environmental challenges. For example, the California Clean Energy Fund (CalCEF) is a nonprofit organization that invests in clean energy startups. CalCEF has helped to accelerate more than 750 startups across 40 programs (New Energy Nexus, 2023), creating jobs and reducing greenhouse gas emissions.

In addition to these examples, impact investing has also been used to address issues such as affordable housing, education, and financial inclusion. These case studies demonstrate the power of impact investing in creating positive change in various sectors.

Impact Investing in the Public Sector

The public sector has a critical role to play in impact investing. Governments can use their resources and regulatory powers to create an enabling environment for impact investing. For example, the UK government has created a social investment tax relief (SITR) scheme that provides tax incentives for individuals who invest in social enterprises.

Governments can also use impact investing to address social and environmental challenges. For example, the Green Investment Bank in the UK was established to invest in renewable energy projects and support the transition to a low-carbon economy.

In addition to these examples, impact investing can also be used to fund public services such as healthcare and education. By leveraging private capital, governments can improve the quality and accessibility of public services while reducing the burden on taxpayers.

Impact Investing in the Private Sector

The private sector has been a driving force behind the growth of impact investing. Private investors can use their capital to support companies creating positive social and environmental impacts. In addition, impact investing can help companies to attract and retain talent, enhance their brand reputation, and improve their bottom line.

One example of a successful impact investment in the private sector is Patagonia. This clothing company has made sustainability a core part of its business model. Patagonia has invested in sustainable agriculture, renewable energy, and fair labor practices. As a result, it has become a leader in the sustainable fashion industry.

Another example is Unilever, a multinational consumer goods company that has made sustainability a key part of its business strategy. Unilever has invested in renewable energy, sustainable agriculture, and water conservation and has set ambitious targets to reduce its environmental impact.

Impact Investing in Philanthropy

Philanthropy has long been a driver of social and environmental change. Impact investing provides philanthropists with a new tool to achieve their goals. Philanthropists can create sustainable solutions to social and environmental challenges by investing in social enterprises and other impact-driven organizations.

One example of a successful impact investment in philanthropy is the Omidyar Network, founded by eBay founder Pierre Omidyar and his wife, Pam Omidyar. The Omidyar Network invests in organizations that create positive social and environmental impacts, including education, financial inclusion, and human rights.

Another example is the Ford Foundation, which has led impact investing for many years. The Ford Foundation has invested in affordable housing, community development, and other initiatives that create positive social impact.

Impact Investing in the Nonprofit Sector

Nonprofit organizations can also benefit from impact investing. By leveraging private capital, nonprofits can expand their impact and achieve their mission more effectively. Impact investing can also help nonprofits to become more financially sustainable and reduce their reliance on traditional fundraising methods.

One example of a successful impact investment in the nonprofit sector is the Robin Hood Foundation, which invests in poverty-fighting organizations in New York City. The Robin Hood Foundation has invested in education, job training, and other initiatives that help to lift people out of poverty.

Another example is the Acumen Fund, which we discussed earlier. Acumen invests in social enterprises that provide essential goods and services to low-income communities in developing countries. Through its investments, Acumen has helped improve millions of people's lives.

Impact investing is a powerful tool to create positive social and environmental change while generating financial returns. By investing in companies and organizations that are creating impact, we can help to address some of the world's most pressing challenges. Whether you are a philanthropist, investor, or nonprofit leader, there are opportunities to get involved in impact investing and make a difference.

Chapter Summary

- Impact investing can create significant social and environmental impact while generating financial returns.
- Successful impact investments include the Acumen Fund, Social Investment Business, and California Clean Energy Fund.
- The public sector can use impact investing to address social and environmental challenges and fund public services.
- The private sector can use impact investing to support sustainable business practices and attract and retain talent.
- Philanthropy can use impact investing to create sustainable solutions to social and environmental challenges.
- Nonprofits can use impact investing in expanding their impact and becoming more financially sustainable.
- Impact investing can help to address issues such as affordable housing, education, and financial inclusion.
- There are opportunities for individuals and organizations to get involved in impact investing and make a difference.

5

IMPACT INVESTING AND SUSTAINABLE DEVELOPMENT GOALS

A tree growing out of a coin, symbolizing the impact investing can have on sustainable development goals, such as reforestation and biodiversity conservation.

I mpact investing is a powerful tool investors can use to address some of the world's most pressing social and environmental challenges. One of the most powerful frameworks for addressing these challenges is the **United Nations' Sustainable Development Goals** (SDGs). The SDGs are 17 goals that aim to end poverty, protect the planet, and ensure prosperity for all. This chapter will explore the relationship between impact investing and the SDGs, focusing on four specific goals: No Poverty, Zero Hunger, Good Health and Well-being, and Quality Education. We will examine how impact investing can help achieve these goals and the opportunities and challenges associated.

Overview of Sustainable Development Goals

The Sustainable Development Goals were adopted by the United Nations in 2015 and are a universal call to action to end poverty, protect the planet, and ensure that all people enjoy peace and prosperity. The 17 goals are interconnected and address a range of issues, including poverty, hunger, health, education, gender equality, clean water and sanitation, affordable and clean energy, decent work and economic growth, industry, innovation and infrastructure, reduced inequalities, sustainable cities and communities, responsible consumption and production, climate action, life below water, life on land, peace, justice, and strong institutions, and partnerships for the goals.

SDG 1: No Poverty

SDG 1 aims to end poverty in all its forms, everywhere. Impact investing can be critical in achieving this goal by providing capital to businesses and organizations working to create economic opportunities for impoverished people. For example, impact investors can invest in microfinance institutions, social enterprises, and other organizations that provide financial services, job training, and other support to low-income communities. Impact investing can also help address the root causes of poverty by investing in businesses that create jobs, improve access to education and healthcare, and promote sustainable economic growth.

SDG 2: Zero Hunger

SDG 2 aims to end hunger, achieve food security and improved nutrition, and promote sustainable agriculture. Impact investing can help achieve this goal by investing in businesses that promote sustainable agriculture, improve food distribution systems, and increase access to nutritious food. Impact investors can also support organizations that provide training and education to farmers, promote sustainable farming practices, and increase access to markets for small-scale farmers.

SDG 3: Good Health and Well-being

SDG 3 aims to ensure healthy lives and promote well-being for all ages. Impact investing can help achieve this goal by investing in businesses that provide healthcare services, develop new medical technologies, and promote healthy lifestyles. Impact investors can also support organizations that provide education and training to healthcare workers, improve access to healthcare in underserved communities, and promote disease prevention and management.

SDG 4: Quality Education

SDG 4 aims to ensure inclusive and equitable education and promote lifelong learning opportunities for all. Impact investing can help achieve this goal by investing in businesses that provide education services, develop new educational technologies, and promote access to education for marginalized communities. Impact investors can also support organizations that provide teacher training, improve access to education in underserved communities, and promote education for girls and women.

. . .

Impact investing can play a significant role in achieving Sustainable Development Goals. By investing in businesses and organizations that are working to address poverty, hunger, health, and education, impact investors can help create positive social and environmental impacts while generating financial returns. However, impact investing has challenges, and investors must carefully consider their investments' social and environmental impact. Nevertheless, impact investors, businesses, and organizations can help create a more sustainable and equitable world by working together.

Chapter Summary

- The Sustainable Development Goals are 17 goals that aim to end poverty, protect the planet, and ensure prosperity for all.
- Impact investing can help achieve the SDGs by providing capital to businesses and organizations working to create positive social and environmental impact.
- Impact investing can help achieve SDG 1 by investing in businesses that create economic opportunities for impoverished people.
- Impact investing can help achieve SDG 2 by investing in businesses that promote sustainable agriculture and increase access to nutritious food.
- Impact investing can help achieve SDG 3 by investing in businesses that provide healthcare services and promote healthy lifestyles.
- Impact investing can help achieve SDG 4 by investing in businesses that provide education services and promote access to education for marginalized communities.
- Impact investing has challenges, and investors must carefully consider their investments' social and environmental impact.
- By working together, impact investors, businesses, and organizations can help create a more sustainable and equitable world.

6

IMPACT INVESTING AND SUSTAINABLE DEVELOPMENT GOALS (CONT.)

A futuristic cityscape powered by sustainable infrastructure, showcasing the impact investing sectors of green buildings, sustainable transportation, and waste management.

I mpact investing is a powerful tool for achieving Sustainable Development Goals (SDGs). The previous chapter discussed how impact investing could contribute to SDGs 1-4. This chapter will explore how impact investing can help achieve SDGs 5-9. These goals are critical for creating a more equitable, sustainable, and prosperous world. By investing in companies and projects that align with these goals, impact investors can drive positive social and environmental change while generating financial returns.

SDG 5: Gender Equality

Gender equality is a fundamental human right for creating a peaceful, prosperous, and sustainable world. Impact investors can play a crucial role in promoting gender equality by investing in companies and projects that empower women and girls. Here are five ways that impact investing can contribute to SDG 5:

Firstly, impact investors can invest in women-led businesses. Women entrepreneurs often face significant barriers to accessing capital, markets, and networks. By investing in women-led businesses, impact investors can help bridge this gap and support positive social and environmental impact.

Secondly, impact investors can support women's health and well-being by investing in companies and projects that provide women access to healthcare, education, and other essential services. This can help improve women's health and well-being, which is critical for achieving gender equality.

Thirdly, impact investors can promote gender diversity and inclusion by encouraging companies to adopt gender diversity and inclusion policies and practices. This can help create a more equitable and inclusive workplace that benefits both women and men.

Fourthly, impact investors can address gender-based violence by investing in companies and projects tackling domestic violence, sexual harassment, and human trafficking. This can help create safer and more secure communities for women and girls.

Finally, impact investors can support women's economic empowerment by investing in companies and projects that provide women with access to financial services, training, and employment opportunities. This can help women achieve economic independence and contribute to their families and communities.

In conclusion, impact investing can be a powerful tool for promoting gender equality. By investing in companies and projects that empower women and girls, impact investors can help create a more just and equitable world.

SDG 6: Clean Water and Sanitation

Access to clean water and sanitation is a fundamental human right and a crucial foundation for sustainable development. Unfortunately, the global water crisis continues to threaten the health and well-being of millions worldwide. However, impact investors can play a vital role in addressing this crisis by investing in companies and projects that promote clean water and sanitation. Here are five ways impact investing can contribute to SDG 6:

Firstly, impact investors can invest in companies and projects that build and maintain water infrastructure, such as water treatment plants, pipelines, and storage facilities. By doing so, they can help ensure that communities have access to clean and safe water.

Secondly, impact investors can invest in companies and projects that promote water conservation, such as efficient irrigation systems, rainwater harvesting, and wastewater reuse. This can reduce water waste and ensure that water resources are used sustainably.

Thirdly, impact investors can invest in companies and projects that address water pollution, such as industrial wastewater treatment, river restoration, and marine conservation. This can help protect water quality and biodiversity.

Fourthly, impact investors can invest in companies and projects providing sanitation access, such as toilets, sewage treatment, and waste management. This can help improve public health and reduce the spread of waterborne diseases.

Lastly, impact investors can invest in water-related entrepreneurship, such as water filtration, desalination, and irrigation technologies. By doing so, they can create new business opportunities and promote innovation in the water sector.

In conclusion, impact investing can be crucial in addressing the global water crisis and promoting sustainable development. By investing in companies and projects promoting clean water and sanitation, impact investors can help ensure everyone has access to these basic human rights.

SDG 7: Affordable and Clean Energy

Access to affordable and clean energy is crucial for achieving sustainable development. Impact investors can significantly accelerate the transition to a low-carbon economy by investing in companies and projects promoting affordable and clean energy. Here are five ways impact investing can contribute to SDG 7:

Firstly, impact investors can invest in companies and projects that generate renewable energy, such as solar, wind, and hydropower. This can help reduce greenhouse gas emissions and promote energy independence. Furthermore, by investing in renewable energy, impact investors can support the development of sustainable energy sources that are both environmentally friendly and cost-effective.

Secondly, impact investors can invest in companies and projects that promote energy efficiency, such as building retrofits, smart grids, and energy storage. This can help reduce energy waste and lower energy costs. By supporting energy efficiency, impact investors can help businesses and households save money on their energy bills while reducing their carbon footprint.

Thirdly, impact investors can invest in companies and projects that provide access to affordable and clean energy for low-income communities, such as off-grid solar systems and mini-grids. This can help reduce energy poverty and improve the quality of life for those who lack access to reliable energy sources. Impact investors can help bridge the energy gap and promote social equity by investing in energy access.

Fourthly, impact investors can invest in companies and projects that promote sustainable transportation, such as electric vehicles, public transit, and bike-sharing. This can help reduce air pollution and traffic congestion, leading to cleaner and healthier cities. By supporting sustainable transportation, impact investors can help create a more sustainable future for urban areas.

Finally, impact investors can invest in energy-related entrepreneurship, such as energy storage, carbon capture, and biofuels. This can create new business opportunities and promote innovation in the energy sector. By supporting energy-related entrepreneurship, impact investors can help drive the development of new technologies and solutions that can help address the challenges of climate change.

In conclusion, impact investing can be critical in promoting sustainable development by investing in companies and projects promoting affordable and clean energy. By investing in renewable energy, energy efficiency, energy access, sustainable transportation, and energy-related entrepreneurship, impact investors can help accelerate the transition to a low-carbon economy and create a more sustainable future for all.

SDG 8: Decent Work and Economic Growth

Decent work and economic growth are crucial for reducing poverty and promoting sustainable development. Impact investors can create decent work and economic growth by investing in companies and projects prioritizing social and environmental sustainability. Here are five ways impact investing can contribute to SDG 8:

Firstly, impact investors can invest in social enterprises that aim to create positive social and environmental impact while generating financial returns. This can help create new jobs and promote sustainable economic growth.

Secondly, impact investors can invest in companies and projects that promote fair labor practices, such as living wages, safe working conditions, and workers' rights. This can help reduce labor exploitation and promote social justice.

Thirdly, impact investors can invest in companies and projects that address income inequality, such as affordable housing, education, and healthcare. This can help reduce poverty and promote economic mobility.

Fourthly, impact investors can invest in companies and projects that promote sustainable supply chains, such as fair trade, organic farming, and responsible mining. This can help reduce environmental degradation and promote social responsibility.

Lastly, impact investors can invest in companies and projects that promote economic development in underserved communities, such as rural areas, indigenous communities, and low-income neighborhoods. This can help reduce economic disparities and promote social inclusion.

In conclusion, impact investing can contribute significantly to SDG 8 by promoting social and environmental sustainability, fair labor practices, income equality, sustainable supply chains, and economic development in underserved communities. By investing in these areas, impact investors can help create decent work and economic growth, reduce poverty and promote sustainable development.

SDG 9: Industry, Innovation, and Infrastructure

Industry, innovation, and infrastructure are critical to promoting sustainable development and economic growth. Impact investors can drive innovation and infrastructure development by investing in companies and projects promoting social and environmental sustainability. Here are five ways impact investing can contribute to SDG 9:

Firstly, impact investors can invest in companies and projects that build and maintain sustainable infrastructure, such as renewable energy, public transit, and green buildings. This can help reduce environmental impact and promote social and economic sustainability.

Secondly, impact investors can invest in companies and projects promoting sustainability innovation, such as clean technology, circular economy, and sustainable agriculture. This can help drive economic growth and environmental sustainability.

Thirdly, impact investors can invest in companies and projects that address the digital divide, such as broadband access, digital literacy, and e-commerce. This can help reduce economic disparities and promote social inclusion.

Fourthly, impact investors can invest in companies and projects that promote sustainable tourism, such as eco-tourism, cultural tourism, and community-based tourism. This can help promote economic development and environmental conservation.

Lastly, impact investors can invest in companies and projects that promote infrastructure development in underserved communities, such as rural areas, indigenous communities, and low-income neighborhoods. This can help reduce economic disparities and promote social inclusion.

Impact investors can help drive sustainable development and economic growth by investing in these areas while promoting social and environmental sustainability.

Impact investing can play a critical role in achieving Sustainable Development Goals. By investing in companies and projects that promote social and environmental sustainability, impact investors can drive positive change while generating financial returns. This chapter explored how impact investing can contribute to SDGs 5-9, which is critical for creating a more equitable, sustainable, and prosperous world.

Chapter Summary

- Impact investing can promote gender equality by investing in women-led businesses, supporting women's health and well-being, promoting gender diversity and inclusion, addressing gender-based violence, and supporting women's economic empowerment.
- Impact investing can address the global water crisis by investing in water infrastructure, supporting water conservation, addressing water pollution, providing access to sanitation, and supporting water-related entrepreneurship.

- Impact investing can accelerate the transition to a low-carbon economy by investing in renewable energy, supporting energy efficiency, addressing energy poverty, promoting sustainable transportation, and supporting energy-related entrepreneurship.
- Impact investing can create decent work and economic growth by investing in social enterprises, supporting fair labor practices, addressing income inequality, promoting sustainable supply chains, and supporting economic development in underserved communities.
- Impact investing can drive innovation and infrastructure development by investing in sustainable infrastructure, supporting innovation for sustainability, addressing the digital divide, promoting sustainable tourism, and supporting infrastructure development in underserved communities.

7

IMPACT INVESTING AND SUSTAINABLE DEVELOPMENT GOALS (CONT.)

A city skyline, with buildings made from sustainable materials and powered by renewable energy, illustrating the transformative impact of impact investing on urban development and climate action.

I mpact investing is a powerful tool that can help achieve the Sustainable Development Goals (SDGs) set by the United Nations. The previous chapter discussed SDGs 5-9 and how to impact investing can contribute to their achievement. This chapter will explore SDGs 10-14 and how to impact investing can help reduce inequalities, create sustainable cities and communities, promote responsible consumption and production, take climate action, and protect life below water. By investing in companies and projects that align with these goals, impact investors can positively impact the world while generating financial returns.

SDG 10: Reduced Inequalities

SDG 10 aims to reduce inequalities within and among countries. This includes reducing income inequality, promoting social, economic, and political inclusion, and ensuring equal opportunities for all. Impact investors can contribute to this goal by investing in companies that promote diversity and inclusion, provide access to education and healthcare, and create job opportunities for marginalized communities. For example, impact investors can invest in microfinance institutions that provide loans to women entrepreneurs or companies that provide affordable housing for low-income families.

Investing in companies that promote diversity and inclusion can also lead to better financial performance. Studies have shown that companies with diverse leadership teams and inclusive cultures outperform their peers. By investing in these companies, impact investors can positively impact society and generate financial returns.

However, impact investors must also be aware of the potential risks of investing in companies that claim to promote diversity and inclusion but do not follow through on their promises. Therefore, it is important to conduct thorough due diligence and ensure that the companies align with the investor's values and goals.

In addition to investing in companies, impact investors can support organizations that advocate for policies promoting equality and inclusion. Using their influence and resources, impact investors can help create a more just and equitable society.

SDG 11: Sustainable Cities and Communities

SDG 11 aims to make cities and human settlements inclusive, safe, resilient, and sustainable. This includes promoting sustainable transportation, reducing air pollution, providing access to affordable housing, and protecting cultural and natural heritage. Impact investors can contribute to this goal by investing in companies that develop sustainable infrastructure, promote renewable energy, and provide affordable housing.

For example, impact investors can invest in companies that develop sustainable transportation solutions such as electric vehicles or public transportation systems. They can also invest in companies that promote renewable energy, such as solar or wind power. As a result, impact investors can help reduce carbon emissions and promote a more sustainable future by investing in these companies.

Investing in affordable housing is also important to promote sustainable cities and communities. For example, impact investors can invest in companies that provide affordable housing for low-income families or organizations that advocate for policies promoting affordable housing. By doing so, impact investors can help reduce homelessness and improve the quality of life for millions of people.

SDG 12: Responsible Consumption and Production

SDG 12 aims to ensure sustainable consumption and production patterns. This includes promoting resource efficiency, reducing waste, and promoting sustainable lifestyles. Impact investors can contribute to this goal by investing in companies that promote sustainable production methods, reduce waste, and develop sustainable products.

For example, impact investors can invest in companies that develop sustainable packaging solutions or in companies that promote circular economy models. They can also invest in companies that develop sustainable agriculture practices or promote sustainable fishing practices. By investing in these companies, impact investors can help reduce waste and promote sustainable consumption and production patterns.

Impact investors can also support organizations that promote sustainable lifestyles and educate consumers about the impact of their choices. By doing so, impact investors can help create a more sustainable future.

SDG 13: Climate Action

SDG 13 aims to take urgent action to combat climate change and its impacts. This includes reducing greenhouse gas emissions, promoting renewable energy, and increasing climate resilience. Impact investors can contribute to this goal by investing in companies that develop renewable energy solutions, promote energy efficiency, and reduce carbon emissions.

For example, impact investors can invest in companies that develop solar or wind power solutions or in companies that promote energy-efficient buildings. They can also invest in companies that develop carbon capture and storage technologies or in companies that promote sustainable transportation solutions. As a result, impact investors can help reduce carbon emissions and promote a more sustainable future by investing in these companies.

Impact investors can also support organizations advocating for climate action policies. Using their influence and resources, impact investors can help create a more sustainable future for all.

SDG 14: Life Below Water

SDG 14 aims to conserve and sustainably use the oceans, seas, and marine resources for sustainable development. This includes reducing marine pollution, protecting marine ecosystems, and promoting sustainable fishing practices. Impact investors can contribute to this goal by investing in companies that promote sustainable fishing practices, reduce marine pollution, and protect marine ecosystems.

For example, impact investors can invest in companies that develop sustainable aquaculture practices or promote sustainable fishing practices. They can also invest in companies that develop technologies to reduce marine pollution or in organizations that advocate for policies that protect marine ecosystems. By investing in these companies, impact investors can help promote sustainable development and protect life below water.

Impact investing can play a crucial role in achieving Sustainable Development Goals. By investing in companies and projects that align with these goals, impact investors can positively impact the world while generating financial returns. This chapter explored how to impact investing can contribute to SDG 10: Reduced Inequalities, SDG 11: Sustainable Cities and Communities, SDG 12: Responsible Consumption and Production, SDG 13: Climate Action, and SDG 14: Life Below Water. Impact investors can help create a more just, equitable, and sustainable world by investing in these areas.

Chapter Summary

- Impact investors can contribute to SDG 10 by investing in companies that promote diversity and inclusion and provide access to education and healthcare.
- Investing in companies promoting diversity and inclusion can improve financial performance.
- Impact investors can support organizations that advocate for policies that promote equality and inclusion.
- Impact investors can contribute to SDG 11 by investing in companies that develop sustainable infrastructure and promote renewable energy.
- Investing in affordable housing is important to promote sustainable cities and communities.

- Impact investors can contribute to SDG 12 by investing in companies that promote sustainable production methods and reduce waste.
- Impact investors can support organizations that promote sustainable lifestyles and educate consumers about the impact of their choices.
- Impact investors can contribute to SDG 13 by investing in companies that develop renewable energy solutions and promote energy efficiency.

8

IMPACT INVESTING AND SUSTAINABLE DEVELOPMENT GOALS (CONT.)

A lightbulb surrounded by a green environment, representing the innovative and sustainable solutions that impact investing can generate to address pressing social and environmental challenges, such as climate change and biodiversity loss.

I mpact investing has emerged as a powerful tool to address the world's most pressing social and environmental challenges. It is a form of investing that seeks to generate measurable social and environmental impact alongside financial returns. This chapter will explore the relationship between impact investing and the Sustainable Development Goals (SDGs), a set of 17 global goals adopted by the United Nations in 2015 to end poverty, protect the planet, and ensure prosperity for all. We will examine how impact investing can contribute to achieving the three remaining SDGs: Life on Land (SDG 15), Peace, Justice and Strong Institutions (SDG 16), and Partnerships for the Goals (SDG 17). We will also discuss the future of sustainable development and the role of governments in promoting impact investing.

SDG 15: Life on Land

SDG 15 aims to protect, restore, and promote the sustainable use of terrestrial ecosystems, sustainably manage forests, combat desertification, and halt and reverse land degradation and biodiversity loss. Impact investing can be crucial in achieving this goal by providing capital to businesses and organizations working to conserve and restore ecosystems, promote sustainable agriculture, and protect biodiversity.

One example of impact investing in SDG 15 is the Rainforest Alliance's certification program, which helps farmers and forest managers adopt sustainable practices that protect ecosystems and improve livelihoods. Impact investors can support this program by investing in companies that produce sustainably produced commodities like coffee, cocoa, and timber. Another example is the Wildlife Conservation Society's Conservation Solutions Fund, which provides grants and loans to conservation entrepreneurs developing innovative solutions to protect wildlife and ecosystems.

Impact investing in SDG 15 can also help address the root causes of deforestation and land degradation, such as poverty and lack of access to finance. In addition, by investing in businesses that provide sustainable livelihoods to local communities, impact investors can help reduce the pressure on forests and other natural resources. For example, Root Capital provides loans and training to small and growing businesses in rural areas, helping them to improve their productivity and sustainability.

In addition to providing capital, impact investors can promote policy and regulatory frameworks supporting sustainable land use. By engaging with governments and other stakeholders, impact investors can advocate for policies that incentivize sustainable practices and discourage destructive activities. For example, the Global Impact Investing Network's Land Use Working Group is working to develop a set of principles for responsible land use investment.

Overall, impact investing can be a powerful tool for achieving SDG 15 by providing capital, promoting sustainable practices, and advocating for policy change.

SDG 16: Peace, Justice, and Strong Institutions

SDG 16 aims to promote peaceful and inclusive societies, provide access to justice for all, and build effective, accountable, and inclusive institutions at all levels. Impact investing can contribute to achieving this goal by supporting businesses and organizations that promote social justice, human rights, and good governance.

One example of impact investing in SDG 16 is the International Finance Corporation's (IFC) Access to Justice program, which provides financing and technical assistance to legal service providers in developing countries. By improving access to justice for marginalized communities, this program helps to promote social justice and human rights. Another example is the Omidyar Network's Governance & Citizen Engagement initiative, which supports organizations that promote transparency, accountability, and citizen participation in government.

Impact investing in SDG 16 can also help build strong and inclusive institutions by providing capital to businesses that promote economic development and job creation. By supporting small and medium-sized enterprises (SMEs) in developing countries, impact investors can help to build a more inclusive economy and reduce poverty. For example, the

African Development Bank's SME Program provides financing and technical assistance to African SMEs, helping them grow and create jobs.

In addition to providing capital, impact investors can promote good governance and accountability. By engaging with governments and other stakeholders, impact investors can advocate for policies that promote transparency, reduce corruption, and strengthen institutions. For example, the Principles for Responsible Investment's (PRI) Engagements on Governance program engages with companies and governments to promote good governance practices.

Overall, impact investing can be a powerful tool for achieving SDG 16 by supporting businesses promoting social justice, human rights, and good governance and advocating for policy change.

SDG 17: Partnerships for the Goals

SDG 17 aims to strengthen the means of implementation and revitalize the global partnership for sustainable development. Impact investing can contribute to achieving this goal by fostering partnerships between investors, businesses, governments, and civil society organizations.

One example of impact investing in SDG 17 is the Global Impact Investing Network's (GIIN) ImpactBase platform. It connects impact investors with investment opportunities that align with their social and environmental goals. By providing a marketplace for impact investments, ImpactBase helps to facilitate partnerships between investors and businesses. Another example is the IFC's Scaling Solar program, which helps governments in developing countries to attract private sector investment in solar energy projects. By bringing together governments, investors, and project developers, this program helps to create partnerships that promote sustainable development.

Impact investing in SDG 17 can also help to build capacity and promote knowledge sharing among stakeholders. By investing in education and training programs, impact investors can build the skills and knowledge needed to promote sustainable development. For example, the Acumen Fund's Lean Data initiative provides training and tools to help social enterprises measure their impact and improve performance.

In addition to fostering partnerships, impact investors can also play a role in promoting innovation and entrepreneurship. By investing in businesses developing innovative solutions to social and environmental challenges, impact investors can help drive progress toward the SDGs. For example, the Unreasonable Group's Unreasonable Impact program supports high-growth companies addressing social and environmental challenges, providing them mentorship, resources, and access to capital.

Overall, impact investing can be a powerful tool for achieving SDG 17 by fostering partnerships, building capacity, promoting innovation, and driving progress toward the SDGs.

Impact Investing and the Future of Sustainable Development

Impact investing can play a significant role in achieving the SDGs and promoting sustainable development more broadly. However, realizing this potential will require continued growth and innovation in the impact investing industry.

One key challenge facing impact investing is the need for more **standardized impact measurement and reporting**. With clear and consistent metrics for measuring social and environmental impact, it can be easier for investors to assess the effectiveness of their investments. The Impact Management Project, a collaborative effort by leading impact investing organizations, is working to develop a set of standardized impact metrics and reporting practices.

Another challenge is the need for more capital to flow into impact investing. While the impact investing industry has grown significantly in recent years, it still represents a small fraction of the overall investment market. To attract more capital, impact investors must demonstrate that they can generate competitive financial returns alongside measurable social and environmental impact.

Finally, impact investing must continue evolving and adapting to social and environmental challenges. As new issues emerge, impact investors must develop new investment strategies and approaches to addressing them. For example, the COVID-19 pandemic has highlighted the need for healthcare, education, and social safety net investments.

Overall, the future of sustainable development will depend in part on the growth and evolution of impact investing. By addressing these challenges and continuing to innovate, impact investors can help to drive progress towards a more sustainable and equitable world.

Impact Investing and the Role of Governments

Governments have a critical role in promoting impact investing and achieving the SDGs. By creating supportive policy and regulatory frameworks, governments can help to unlock private sector capital and promote sustainable development.

One key policy tool for promoting impact investing is **tax incentives.** Governments can encourage more capital to flow into the impact investing industry by providing tax breaks for impact investments. For example, the UK government's Social Investment Tax Relief program provides tax breaks for investments in social enterprises.

Another important policy tool is public-private partnerships. Governments can leverage private sector expertise and resources to achieve social and environmental goals by partnering with the private sector. For example, the US government's Power Africa initiative is a public-private partnership that aims to increase access to electricity in sub-Saharan Africa by mobilizing private sector investment.

In addition to creating supportive policy frameworks, governments can promote impact investing through their investments. By investing in impact funds and supporting impact-oriented businesses, governments can demonstrate the viability and potential of impact investing. For example, the French government's Bpifrance invests in impact funds and provides financing to impact-oriented businesses.

Overall, governments are critical in promoting impact investing and achieving the SDGs. By creating supportive policy frameworks, partnering with the private sector, and investing in impact-oriented businesses, governments can help to unlock private sector capital and drive progress towards a more sustainable and equitable world.

Chapter Summary

- Impact investing can contribute to achieving SDG 15 by providing capital, promoting sustainable practices, and advocating for policy change.
- Impact investing can contribute to achieving SDG 16 by supporting businesses that promote social justice, human rights, and good governance and advocating for policy change.
- Impact investing can contribute to achieving SDG 17 by fostering partnerships, building capacity, promoting innovation, and driving progress toward the SDGs.
- The future of sustainable development will depend in part on the growth and evolution of impact investing, including the development of standardized impact metrics, the attraction of more capital, and the adaptation to new challenges.
- Governments are critical in promoting impact investing and achieving the SDGs through tax incentives, public-private partnerships, and investments in impact-oriented businesses.

9

IMPACT INVESTING AND SOCIAL ENTREPRENEURSHIP

A vibrant city street, with storefronts that showcase different impact investing initiatives, from sustainable fashion boutiques to eco-friendly cafes and community gardens.

Social entrepreneurship and impact investing are two concepts that have gained significant attention in recent years. They aim to create positive social and environmental impact while generating financial returns. In this chapter, we will explore the definition of social entrepreneurship, its relationship with impact investing, different social entrepreneurship models, the role of innovation in social entrepreneurship, and the importance of sustainability.

Definition of Social Entrepreneurship

Social entrepreneurship is a dynamic and multifaceted concept that has gained significant traction recently. It is a term that refers to the practice of creating innovative solutions to social and environmental problems. Social entrepreneurs use their creativity, passion, and business acumen to address social and environmental challenges. They are driven by a desire to create positive change and improve the lives of people and communities.

Social entrepreneurship is not limited to any particular sector or industry. It can take many forms, including nonprofits, for-profits, and hybrid organizations. Social entrepreneurs are found in various fields, including healthcare, education, energy, and agriculture. They are united by their commitment to creating sustainable solutions that can be scaled and replicated to address systemic social and environmental challenges.

One of the key differences between social entrepreneurship and traditional entrepreneurship is the prioritization of social and environmental impact over financial returns. While traditional entrepreneurs primarily focus on generating profits, social entrepreneurs measure success by the bottom line and the positive impact they create. In addition, they are committed to creating sustainable solutions that can be scaled and replicated to address systemic social and environmental challenges.

Social entrepreneurship is a powerful force for positive change in the world. It has the potential to transform the way we think about business and the role it can play in creating a better world. Social entrepreneurs are creating a more just, equitable, and sustainable future for all by harnessing the power of innovation, creativity, and business acumen.

Social Entrepreneurship and Impact Investing

Social entrepreneurship and impact investing are two concepts that have gained significant traction in recent years. Both focus on creating positive social and environmental impact but approach this goal differently. Social entrepreneurship is using business principles to solve social and environmental problems. Impact investing, on the other hand, is a form of investing that seeks to generate social and environmental impact alongside financial returns.

Impact investors are individuals or organizations that invest in social enterprises, nonprofits, and other organizations committed to creating positive social and environmental impact. Unlike traditional investors, impact investors prioritize impact over financial returns. As a result, they accept lower financial returns in exchange for knowing that their investments make a positive difference.

Social entrepreneurs often rely on impact investors to fund their ventures. These investors provide social entrepreneurs the capital they need to scale their solutions and create greater impact. Impact investors also provide social entrepreneurs the expertise and resources they need to succeed. In addition, they may offer guidance on business strategy, marketing, and other key areas, as well as connections to other investors and potential partners.

One of the key benefits of impact investing is that it allows investors to **align their investments with their values.** In addition, by investing in organizations that are working to create positive social and environmental impact, impact investors can feel good about the impact their money is making. This can especially appeal to younger investors looking to make a positive difference.

Social entrepreneurship and impact investing are powerful tools for creating positive social and environmental impact. Social entrepreneurs and impact investors can create innovative solutions to some of the world's most pressing problems by working together. Whether it's addressing climate change, reducing poverty, or improving access to healthcare, social entrepreneurship, and impact investing have the potential to make a real difference in the world.

Social Entrepreneurship Models

Social entrepreneurship is a rapidly growing field that seeks to address social and environmental issues through innovative business models. There are several different social entrepreneurship models, each with strengths and weaknesses. These models include nonprofits, for-profits, and hybrid organizations.

Nonprofits are organizations dedicated to a social or environmental mission and do not distribute profits to shareholders. As a result, they are often better suited for addressing immediate social and environmental needs, such as providing food and shelter to those in need or responding to natural disasters. Instead, nonprofits rely on donations and grants to fund their operations. As a result, their impact on their target population often measures their success.

On the other hand, for-profits aim to generate financial returns while also creating social and environmental impact. As a result, they are often better suited for creating sustainable solutions that can be scaled and replicated, such as developing new technologies or business models that address social and environmental issues. For-profits rely on revenue from their products or services to fund their operations. Their success is often measured by their financial performance and social and environmental impact.

Hybrid organizations combine elements of both nonprofits and for-profits. They seek to create social and environmental impact while generating financial returns and often have a dual bottom line. Hybrid organizations can take many forms, such as social enterprises, benefit corporations, or community interest companies. They face unique challenges in balancing their social and financial goals. Their success is often measured by their ability to achieve both.

Overall, social entrepreneurship models offer a range of options for addressing social and environmental issues. Each model has its strengths and weaknesses, and the choice of model will depend on the specific goals and needs of the organization. Nevertheless, by leveraging the power of business to create positive social and environmental impact, social entrepreneurship can transform how we address some of the world's most pressing challenges.

Social Entrepreneurship and Innovation

Social entrepreneurship is a rapidly growing field that combines business principles with social and environmental goals. It allows individuals and organizations to create positive change in the world while generating revenue and creating sustainable solutions. One of the key components of social entrepreneurship is innovation, which is used to create new solutions to complex social and environmental challenges.

Innovation is essential for social entrepreneurs because it allows them to constantly experiment and iterate until they find the most effective and sustainable solutions. This process can take many forms, including developing new technologies, business models, and partnerships. As a result, social entrepreneurs can create more efficient, effective, and impactful solutions by embracing innovation.

In addition to creating new solutions, social entrepreneurs also use innovation to develop new funding models. For example, crowdfunding, impact investing, and social impact bonds are all innovative funding models that have emerged in recent years. These models provide social entrepreneurs with new sources of capital and allow them to scale their solutions more quickly.

Crowdfunding is a popular funding model that allows social entrepreneurs to raise money from many people through online platforms. This model is particularly effective for projects with a strong social or environmental mission, as it allows individuals to contribute small amounts of money to support a cause they believe in.

Impact investing is another innovative funding model that has recently gained popularity. This model involves investing in companies or organizations with a social or environmental mission to generate financial returns and positive social impact. Impact investors are looking for companies that are creating positive change in the world and are willing to invest in them to help them grow and scale their impact.

Social impact bonds are a more complex funding model that involves private investors providing upfront capital to fund social programs. If the program successfully achieves its goals, the investors receive a return on their investment. This model is particularly effective for programs with a measurable impact, as it allows investors to see a direct return on their investment.

Overall, innovation is a critical component of social entrepreneurship. Social entrepreneurs can create more effective and sustainable solutions to complex social and environmental challenges by embracing new technologies, business models, and funding models. As the field of social entrepreneurship continues to grow, we will see even more innovative solutions emerge in the years to come.

Social Entrepreneurship and Sustainability

Social entrepreneurship is a rapidly growing field gaining recognition for its ability to create innovative solutions to some of the world's most pressing social and environmental challenges. One of the key components of social entrepreneurship is sustainability, which refers to the ability of a solution to be maintained over the long term.

Sustainability is a multifaceted concept encompassing environmental, social, and financial sustainability. Social entrepreneurs recognize that their solutions must be environmentally sustainable to minimize their impact on the planet and ensure that future generations can continue to benefit from them. This means they must consider the entire lifecycle of their products or services, from production to disposal, and strive to minimize waste and pollution at every stage.

In addition to environmental sustainability, social entrepreneurs also prioritize social sustainability. This means their solutions must be designed to create a positive social impact over the long term. They must consider the needs and perspectives of all stakeholders, including the communities they serve, and work to build relationships based on trust and mutual respect. Social entrepreneurs must also ensure their solutions are culturally appropriate and sensitive to local customs and traditions.

Finally, social entrepreneurs must ensure that their solutions are financially sustainable. This means that they must be able to generate the revenue they need to sustain their operations over the long term. Therefore, they must develop business models that are financially viable, scalable, and adapt to changing market conditions. Social entrepreneurs must also be able to measure and communicate their solutions' social and environmental impact to attract funding and support from investors and other stakeholders.

In summary, sustainability is a critical component of social entrepreneurship. Social entrepreneurs must create environmentally, socially, and financially sustainable solutions to address systemic social and environmental challenges. Social entrepreneurs can create lasting impact by prioritizing sustainability and contributing to a more equitable and sustainable world.

Social entrepreneurship and impact investing are powerful tools for creating positive social and environmental impact. They desire to create sustainable solutions that can be scaled and replicated to address systemic social and environmental challenges. Social entrepreneurship and impact investing are not just about generating financial returns; they are about creating a better world for all.

Chapter Summary

- Social entrepreneurship is creating innovative solutions to social and environmental problems.
- Impact investing seeks to generate social and environmental impact alongside financial returns.
- Several social entrepreneurship models exist, including nonprofits, for-profits, and hybrid organizations.
- Innovation is a critical component of social entrepreneurship.

- Sustainability is another critical component of social entrepreneurship.
- Social entrepreneurs aim to create environmentally, socially, and financially sustainable solutions.
- Social entrepreneurs must ensure that their solutions are financially viable and can generate the revenue they need to sustain their operations.
- Social entrepreneurs must also ensure that their solutions are socially sustainable and can create a positive social impact over the long term.

10

IMPACT INVESTING AND CORPORATE SOCIAL RESPONSIBILITY

A tree with roots made of coins and leaves made of hearts, symbolizing the positive impact of impact investing and corporate social responsibility on the environment and society.

I n today's world, businesses are about more than just making profits. They are also expected to contribute to society and the environment. This is where Corporate Social Responsibility (CSR) comes into play. CSR is a concept that has gained immense popularity in recent years. It refers to the responsibility of businesses towards society and the environment. Impact investing, on the other hand, is a relatively new concept that aims to generate social and environmental impact along with financial returns. This chapter will explore the relationship between CSR and impact investing and how they can work together to create a better world.

Definition of Corporate Social Responsibility

Corporate Social Responsibility (CSR) is a concept that refers to the responsibility of businesses toward society and the environment. Businesses take a voluntary initiative to go beyond their legal obligations and contribute to society. CSR involves considering business operations' social, environmental, and economic impacts and making decisions that benefit all stakeholders, including employees, customers, suppliers, communities, and the environment.

CSR is **not just about philanthropy or charity**. We are integrating social and environmental considerations into business operations and decision-making processes. As a result, CSR can help businesses build a positive reputation, attract and retain customers and employees, and create long-term value for all stakeholders.

Corporate Social Responsibility and Impact Investing

Corporate Social Responsibility (CSR) and Impact Investing are two concepts that have gained significant attention in recent years. CSR refers to the responsibility that businesses have towards society and the environment. It involves taking actions that benefit society and the environment beyond the legal requirements. Impact investing, on the other hand, is a relatively new concept that aims to generate social and environmental impact and financial returns.

Impact investors invest in businesses that have a positive social or environmental impact. These businesses are often referred to as social enterprises or impact-driven businesses. Impact investing can be seen as a form of CSR, as it involves businesses taking responsibility for their impact on society and the environment.

The concept of shared value is central to both CSR and impact investing. Shared value refers to the idea that businesses can create value for themselves and society at the same time. By investing in businesses that have a positive impact, impact investors can help create a better world while also generating financial returns.

Impact investing has gained significant momentum in recent years, with more and more investors looking to invest in businesses with a positive impact. This has led to the growth of impact-driven businesses and the development of new financial instruments, such as social impact bonds and green bonds.

In conclusion, CSR and impact investing are two concepts that are closely related. Both involve businesses taking responsibility for their impact on society and the environment. Impact investing can help businesses create shared value, where financial, social, and environmental value is created. By investing in businesses that have a positive impact, impact investors can help create a better world while also generating financial returns.

Corporate Social Responsibility Models

Corporate Social Responsibility (CSR) is a concept that has gained significant attention in recent years. It refers to the responsibility of businesses to operate in a manner that benefits society and the environment in addition to generating profits. Businesses can adopt several CSR models, each with its unique approach to achieving this goal.

The **philanthropic model** is one of the most common CSR models. It involves businesses donating money or resources to charitable causes. Businesses often use this model to give back to the community and improve their public image. By supporting charitable causes, businesses can demonstrate their commitment to social responsibility and build goodwill with their customers and stakeholders.

Another popular CSR model is the **stakeholder model**. This model involves businesses considering the interests of all stakeholders, including employees, customers, suppliers, communities, and the environment. The stakeholder model recognizes that businesses are responsible for balancing the needs of all stakeholders, not just shareholders. By taking a stakeholder approach, businesses can build stronger relationships with their stakeholders, improve their reputation, and create a more sustainable business model.

The shared value model is a relatively new CSR model that recently gained popularity. This model involves businesses creating value for themselves, society, and the environment. The shared value model recognizes that businesses can create economic value by addressing social and environmental challenges. By creating shared value, businesses can improve their competitiveness while contributing to the greater good.

In conclusion, businesses can adopt several CSR models, each with its unique approach to achieving social responsibility. For example, the philanthropic model involves businesses donating money or resources to charitable causes. In contrast, the stakeholder model involves businesses considering the interests of all stakeholders. Finally, the shared value model involves businesses creating value for themselves, society, and the environment. By adopting these models, businesses can demonstrate their commitment to social responsibility, build stronger relationships with their stakeholders, and create a more sustainable business model.

Corporate Social Responsibility and Innovation

Corporate Social Responsibility (CSR) is a concept that has gained significant attention in recent years. It refers to the responsibility of businesses to operate in a manner that is ethical, sustainable, and beneficial to society. CSR involves considering the impact of business operations on the environment, employees, customers, and the wider community. One way that businesses can demonstrate their commitment to CSR is through innovation.

Innovation is creating new ideas, products, or services that add value to society. It involves taking risks, experimenting with new approaches, and challenging the status quo. Innovation can play a crucial role in CSR by enabling businesses to create products or services with a positive social or environmental impact. For example, a company might develop a new technology that reduces carbon emissions or a product made from sustainable materials.

Innovation can also help businesses to reduce their environmental footprint or improve the working conditions of their employees. For example, a company might develop a new manufacturing process that uses less energy or a new system for tracking employee health and safety. By investing in innovation. As a result, businesses can improve their operations and demonstrate their commitment to CSR.

Moreover, innovation can help businesses to create new markets or opportunities. By addressing social or environmental challenges, businesses can tap into new markets or create new products or services that meet the needs of consumers. For example, a company might develop a new product to address a specific social or environmental issue, such as reducing plastic waste or improving access to clean water.

In conclusion, innovation and CSR are closely linked. By investing in innovation, businesses can create products or services with a positive social or environmental impact, reduce their environmental footprint, improve working conditions, and create new markets or opportunities. As such, businesses prioritizing innovation as part of their CSR strategy will likely be more successful in the long run.

Corporate Social Responsibility and Sustainability

Corporate Social Responsibility (CSR) and Sustainability are two intertwined concepts that have become increasingly important in business. Sustainability, in particular, has become a key aspect of CSR as businesses are now expected to take responsibility for their impact on the environment and society.

In today's world, businesses are expected not only to generate profits but also to operate sustainably. This means that they must ensure that their operations do not harm the environment and take steps to reduce their carbon footprint. This involves adopting sustainable practices such as using renewable energy sources, reducing waste, and conserving natural resources.

Sustainability is not just about being environmentally friendly; it also has economic and social benefits. By adopting sustainable practices, businesses can reduce costs, improve their reputation, and attract and retain customers and employees. For example, businesses that use renewable energy sources can reduce their energy bills. In contrast, those that reduce waste can save on disposal costs.

Moreover, sustainability can help businesses create long-term value. By investing in sustainable practices, businesses can future-proof their operations and ensure longevity. In addition, sustainable practices are often more efficient and cost-effective in the long run. Finally, they can help businesses adapt to changing market conditions.

In conclusion, sustainability is a crucial aspect of CSR. Businesses must take responsibility for their impact on the environment and society. By adopting sustainable practices, businesses can reduce their environmental footprint, create long-term value, and improve their reputation.

CSR and impact investing are two concepts that can work together to create a better world. Businesses can create shared value and generate positive social and environmental impact and financial returns by taking responsibility for their impact on society and the environment. In addition, by adopting sustainable practices and innovating, businesses can create long-term value and contribute to a more sustainable future.

Chapter Summary

- CSR refers to the responsibility of businesses towards society and the environment.

- Impact investing aims to generate social and environmental impact and financial returns.
- CSR and impact investing can work together to create shared value.
- The philanthropic, stakeholder, and shared value models are common models of CSR.
- Innovation can play a crucial role in CSR.
- Sustainability is a key aspect of CSR.
- Adopting sustainable practices can help businesses create long-term value.
- CSR and impact investing can contribute to a more sustainable and equitable future.

11

IMPACT INVESTING AND ETHICAL INVESTING

A ripple effect spreading out from a single drop in a pond, representing the positive impact that impact investing and corporate social responsibility can have on society and the world as a whole.

A s the world becomes more aware of the impact of businesses on society and the environment, ethical investing has become a popular way for investors to align their values with their financial goals. Impact investing takes this a step further by actively seeking out investments that positively impact society and the environment. This chapter will explore the definitions of ethical and impact investing, the different models of ethical investing, and how ethical investing can drive innovation and sustainability.

Definition of Ethical Investing

Ethical investing, also known as socially responsible investing (SRI), is investing in companies that align with an investor's values and beliefs. This can include avoiding companies that engage in activities such as tobacco, weapons, or fossil fuels or investing in companies that prioritize diversity, human rights, and environmental sustainability. Ethical investing can also involve engaging with companies to encourage them to adopt more responsible practices.

Ethical investing has become increasingly popular in recent years, with more investors looking to align their investments with their values. According to a Global Sustainable Investment Alliance report, sustainable investing assets reached $30.7 trillion in 2018, a 34% increase from 2016.

Ethical Investing and Impact Investing

In today's world, investing is not just about making money but also about making a difference. Ethical investing and impact investing are two approaches that have gained popularity in recent years. While both aim to align investments with personal values, their approach, and objectives differ.

Ethical investing is a strategy that focuses on avoiding harm by investing in companies that meet certain ethical standards. This may include avoiding investments in companies that engage in activities such as tobacco, weapons, or animal testing. In addition, ethical investors seek to align their investments with their values and beliefs, often prioritizing social responsibility over financial returns.

On the other hand, impact investing seeks to actively create positive change by investing in companies, organizations, and funds with a measurable social or environmental impact. Impact investors aim to generate financial returns while positively impacting issues such as climate change, poverty, and inequality. They seek to use their investments as a tool for social and environmental change.

The impact investing market has grown significantly in recent years, with many investors looking to make a positive impact with their investments. According to the Global Impact Investing Network, analysts estimated the size of the impact investing market to be $715 billion in 2020. This growth is driven by a growing awareness of the need for sustainable and socially responsible investments and a desire to positively impact the world.

In conclusion, ethical investing and impact investing are two approaches that aim to align investments with personal values and beliefs. While ethical investing focuses on avoiding harm, impact investing seeks to create positive change actively. As the impact investing market continues to grow, investors have the opportunity to make a positive impact on the world while also generating financial returns.

Ethical Investing Models

Ethical investing has become increasingly popular as investors seek to align their financial goals with their values. Investors can choose from several models of ethical investing, each with its unique approach to promoting responsible investment practices.

One of the most common models of ethical investing is **negative screening**. This approach involves avoiding investments in companies that engage in harmful or unethical activities. For example, investors may avoid investing in companies that produce tobacco products and weapons or engage in environmentally damaging practices.

On the other hand, positive screening involves actively seeking out investments in companies that prioritize environmental, social, and governance (ESG) factors. This approach identifies companies committed to sustainable business practices, such as reducing their carbon footprint, promoting diversity and inclusion, and prioritizing employee well-being.

Another model of ethical investing is shareholder advocacy. This approach involves engaging with companies to encourage them to adopt more responsible practices. For example, shareholders may use their voting power to push for company policy or practice changes. In addition, they may engage in dialogue with company management to encourage them to take action on issues such as climate change, human rights, or social justice.

Overall, ethical investing models offer investors a range of options for aligning their investments with their values. For example, investing in companies prioritizing ESG factors or engaging in shareholder advocacy can help promote positive change and contribute to a more sustainable and responsible global economy.

Ethical Investing and Innovation

Ethical investing has become an increasingly popular trend in recent years as more and more investors seek to align their financial goals with their values. This approach to investing involves selecting companies that prioritize environmental, social, and governance (ESG) factors, such as sustainability, diversity, and transparency. By investing in these companies, investors can earn a return on their investment and support businesses that positively impact society and the environment.

One of the key benefits of ethical investing is that it can drive innovation by encouraging companies to adopt more sustainable and responsible practices. When investors demand that companies prioritize ESG factors, it creates a market for sustainable products and services. This, in turn, can lead to increased innovation in areas such as renewable energy, sustainable agriculture, and green transportation.

For example, companies prioritizing sustainability may invest in research and development to create more efficient and eco-friendly products. This could include developing new solar power, wind energy, or electric vehicle technologies. Investing in these companies can support these innovations and contribute to a more sustainable future.

Furthermore, ethical investing can positively impact society by promoting social responsibility and diversity. Companies prioritizing ESG factors are likelier to have diverse leadership teams and inclusive workplace cultures. This can lead to better decision-making, improved employee morale, and a stronger commitment to social responsibility.

In conclusion, ethical investing is a way to align your financial goals with your values and drive innovation and promote positive social and environmental change. Investing in companies prioritizing ESG factors can help create a market for sustainable products and services, support innovative companies, and contribute to a more sustainable and equitable future.

Ethical Investing and Sustainability

Ethical investing is a concept that has gained significant traction in recent years as more and more investors are looking to align their investments with their values. At its core, ethical investing is about investing in companies that prioritize sustainability and social responsibility while avoiding those that engage in harmful practices to the environment or society.

One of the key benefits of ethical investing is its **potential to promote sustainability.** Investing in companies prioritizing sustainability can help create a market for sustainable products and services. This, in turn, can lead to increased adoption of sustainable practices and technologies, which can help mitigate the impacts of climate change and promote a more sustainable future.

Moreover, ethical investing can also encourage companies to adopt more responsible practices. When investors choose to invest in companies that prioritize sustainability, they are sending a clear message to those companies that sustainability is important to them. This can incentivize companies to adopt more sustainable practices to attract ethical investors and remain competitive.

In addition, ethical investing can also have a positive impact on society. Investing in companies prioritizing social responsibility can help support initiatives promoting social justice, human rights, and equality. This can help create a more just and equitable society where everyone can access the resources and opportunities needed to thrive.

Ethical investing is a powerful tool for promoting sustainability and social responsibility. Investing in companies prioritizing these values can help create a more sustainable and equitable future for all.

Ethical and impact investing are powerful tools for investors who want to align their values with their financial goals. By investing in companies that prioritize ESG factors and positively impact society and the environment, investors can help create a more sustainable and equitable world.

Chapter Summary

- Ethical investing involves investing in companies that align with an investor's values and beliefs.
- Impact investing seeks to actively create positive change in climate change, poverty, and inequality.
- Ethical investing models include negative screening, positive screening, and shareholder advocacy.
- Ethical investing can drive innovation by encouraging companies to adopt more sustainable and responsible practices.
- Ethical investing can promote sustainability by encouraging companies to adopt more responsible practices.
- Sustainable investing assets reached $30.7 trillion in 2018, a 34% increase from 2016.
- Analysts estimated the impact investing market to be $715 billion in 2020.
- Ethical and impact investing are powerful tools for investors who want to align their values with their financial goals.

12

IMPACT INVESTING AND THE FUTURE OF INVESTING

A hand holding a sapling, surrounded by symbols of progress and innovation, representing the power of impact investing to cultivate sustainable growth and build a better future.

I mpact investing is a relatively new concept that has gained significant traction recently. It is an investment approach that seeks to generate both financial returns and positive social and environmental impact. As a result, impact investing has the potential to transform the way we invest and create a more sustainable and equitable future. In this chapter, we will explore the trends in impact investing, its impact on the global economy and the financial industry, and the role of investors and consumers in driving this movement forward.

Trends in Impact Investing

Impact investing has grown significantly in recent years, with assets under management reaching over $715 billion in 2020. This growth is driven by several trends, including the increasing demand for sustainable and socially responsible investments, the rise of impact-focused funds and platforms, and the growing awareness of the need to address global challenges such as climate change and inequality.

One of the key trends in impact investing is the focus on **measurable impact.** As a result, investors are increasingly looking for investments that can demonstrate a clear and measurable social or environmental impact. This has led to the development of impact measurements and management frameworks, such as the Impact Management Project and the Global Impact Investing Network's IRIS+ system.

Another trend is the rise of impact-focused funds and platforms. These funds and platforms are dedicated to investing in companies and projects with a positive social or environmental impact. Examples include the Global Impact Investing Network, the Impact Investing Institute, and the Impact Investment Exchange.

Impact investing is also becoming more mainstream, with traditional financial institutions and asset managers entering the space. This is driven by the increasing demand from clients for sustainable and socially responsible investments and the potential for financial returns.

However, there are also challenges to the growth of impact investing, such as the need for more standardization in impact measurement and management and the difficulty in finding suitable investment opportunities that meet both financial and impact criteria.

Impact Investing and the Global Economy

Impact investing can significantly address global challenges such as climate change, poverty, and inequality. By investing in companies and projects that have a positive social or environmental impact, impact investors can help to create a more sustainable and equitable future.

One area where impact investing can significantly impact is the transition to a **low-carbon economy**. By investing in renewable energy, energy efficiency, and other climate solutions, impact investors can help to accelerate the transition to a more sustainable energy system.

Impact investing can also help to address poverty and inequality by investing in companies and projects that provide access to basic services such as healthcare, education, and financial services. This can help to create more inclusive and equitable societies.

However, impact investing alone cannot solve these global challenges. It needs to be part of a broader effort that includes policy changes, technological innovation, and social and cultural shifts.

Impact Investing and the Financial Industry

Impact investing transforms the financial industry by creating new investment opportunities and changing investors' thinking about risk and return. It also drives innovation in impact measurement and management, creating new business models that combine financial and impact objectives.

Impact investing changes the financial industry by creating new investment opportunities. Impact investors invest in companies and projects that traditional investors may overlook, such as social enterprises and community development projects. This is creating new sources of capital for these types of organizations and helping to drive innovation and growth.

Impact investing is also changing the way investors think about risk and return. For example, impact investors are willing to accept lower financial returns in exchange for a positive social or environmental impact. This challenges the traditional view that financial returns are the only measure of investment success.

Finally, impact investing is driving innovation in impact measurement and management. Impact investors are developing new frameworks and tools to measure and manage their investments' social and environmental impact. This is helping to create a more standardized and transparent approach to impact investing.

Impact Investing and the Role of Investors

Investors play a critical role in driving the growth of impact investing. They can use their capital to support companies and projects with a positive social or environmental impact and advocate for policy changes that support impact investing.

Investors can support impact investing by investing in impact-focused funds and platforms. These funds and platforms are dedicated to investing in companies and projects with a positive social or environmental impact. By investing in these funds and platforms, investors can support impact investing growth and help create a more sustainable and equitable future.

Investors can also advocate for policy changes that support impact investing. This can include changes to tax policies, regulations, and government procurement policies supporting impact investing growth.

Finally, investors can use their influence to encourage companies to adopt more sustainable and socially responsible practices. This can include engaging with companies on climate change, human rights, and diversity and inclusion issues.

Impact Investing and the Role of Consumers

Consumers also play a critical role in driving the growth of impact investing. They can use their purchasing power to support companies with a positive social or environmental impact and advocate for policy changes that support impact investing.

Consumers can support impact investing by buying products and services from companies with a positive social or environmental impact. This can include products made from sustainable materials or services that support local communities.

Consumers can also advocate for policy changes that support impact investing. This can include changes to tax policies, regulations, and government procurement policies supporting impact investing growth.

Finally, consumers can use their influence to encourage companies to adopt more sustainable and socially responsible practices. This can include engaging with companies on climate change, human rights, and diversity and inclusion issues.

Impact investing can transform our investment and create a more sustainable and equitable future. It is driven by several trends, including the increasing demand for sustainable and socially responsible investments, the rise of impact-focused funds and platforms, and the growing awareness of the need to address global challenges such as climate change and inequality. However, there are also challenges to the growth of impact investing, such as the need for more standardization in impact measurement and management and the difficulty in finding suitable investment opportunities that meet both financial and impact criteria. In addition, investors and consumers play a critical role in driving the growth of impact investing. By working together, we can create a more sustainable and equitable future.

Chapter Summary

- Impact investing has grown significantly in recent years, driven by the increasing demand for sustainable and socially responsible investments.

- The focus on measurable impact and the rise of impact-focused funds and platforms are key trends in impact investing.
- Impact investing has the potential to address global challenges such as climate change, poverty, and inequality.
- Impact investing transforms the financial industry by creating new investment opportunities and changing investors' thinking about risk and return.
- Investors can support impact investing by investing in impact-focused funds and platforms and advocating for policy changes that support impact investing.
- Consumers can support impact investing by buying products and services from companies with a positive social or environmental impact and advocating for policy changes supporting impact investing.
- Impact investing faces challenges like more standardization in impact measurement and management.
- Impact investing must be part of a broader effort that includes policy changes, technological innovation, and social and cultural shifts to address global challenges.

13

IMPACT INVESTING RESOURCES

A hand planting a seedling in a pot, symbolizing the potential of impact investing to foster sustainable agriculture and food systems, which are critical for achieving the Sustainable Development Goals related to hunger and poverty.

I mpact investing is a rapidly growing field that attracts investors who want to impact society while earning a financial return positively. However, finding the right resources to navigate this complex field can be challenging. This chapter will explore the top impact investing organizations, publications, conferences, events, networks, communities, and tools that can help you make informed investment decisions and maximize your impact.

Impact Investing Organizations

Impact investing organizations are dedicated to promoting and facilitating impact investing. They provide various services, including research, education, networking, and investment opportunities. Here are five of the top impact investing organizations:

1. **Global Impact Investing Network (GIIN):** The GIIN is a nonprofit organization that works to increase the scale and effectiveness of impact investing. They provide research, tools, and resources to help investors and organizations make informed investment decisions.

2. **ImpactAssets:** ImpactAssets is a nonprofit organization that offers impact investing solutions for individuals, families, and institutions. They provide access to various impact investment opportunities, including private debt and equity, public equity, and fixed income.

3. **Acumen:** Acumen is a nonprofit organization that invests in companies working to solve some of the world's most pressing social and environmental problems. They provide patient capital, management support, and strategic advice to help these companies grow and succeed.

4. **B Lab:** B Lab is a nonprofit organization that certifies companies that meet rigorous social and environmental performance standards, accountability, and transparency.

They also provide tools and resources to help companies measure and improve their impact.

5. **Toniic:** Toniic is a global network of impact investors committed to using their capital to create positive social and environmental change. They provide various services, including education, networking, and investment opportunities.

Impact Investing Publications:

Impact investing publications provide valuable insights and information about the field's latest trends, best practices, and success stories. Here are five of the top impact investing publications:

1. **ImpactAlpha:** ImpactAlpha is a digital media platform that covers the latest news and trends in impact investing. They provide in-depth analysis, expert commentary, and various resources for impact investors.

2. **Stanford Social Innovation Review (SSIR):** SSIR is a quarterly magazine that covers the latest trends and best practices in social innovation and impacts investing. They provide insights from leading experts, case studies, and practical tools for social entrepreneurs and impact investors.

3. **NextBillion:** NextBillion is a digital media platform that covers the latest news and trends in social entrepreneurship, impact investing, and sustainable business. They provide insights from leading experts, case studies, and practical tools for social entrepreneurs and impact investors.

4. **Impact Investing Insights:** Impact Investing Insights is a monthly newsletter that provides insights and analysis on the latest trends and best practices in impact investing. They cover various topics, including impact measurement, social entrepreneurship, and sustainable finance.

5. **The Economist:** The Economist is a weekly magazine covering the latest business, finance, and economics news and

trends. They provide in-depth analysis and expert commentary on the impact investing landscape.

Impact Investing Conferences and Events

Impact investing conferences and events provide valuable opportunities to network with other impact investors, learn about the latest trends and best practices, and explore new investment opportunities. Here are five of the top impact investing conferences and events:

1. **SOCAP:** SOCAP is an annual conference that brings together impact investors, social entrepreneurs, and other stakeholders to explore new investment opportunities and share best practices. They provide a range of sessions, workshops, and networking opportunities.

2. **Skoll World Forum:** The Skoll World Forum is an annual conference that brings together social entrepreneurs, impact investors, and other stakeholders to explore new solutions to the world's most pressing social and environmental problems. They provide a range of sessions, workshops, and networking opportunities.

3. **Global Impact Investing Network Investor Forum:** The GIIN Investor Forum is an annual conference that gathers impact investors worldwide to share best practices, explore new investment opportunities, and build relationships.

4. **Social Finance Forum:** The Social Finance Forum is an annual conference that brings together impact investors, social entrepreneurs, and other stakeholders to explore new solutions to social and environmental problems. They provide a range of sessions, workshops, and networking opportunities.

5. **Impact Summit:** The Impact Summit is an annual conference that brings together impact investors, social entrepreneurs, and other stakeholders to explore new investment opportunities and share best practices. They provide a range of sessions, workshops, and networking opportunities.

Impact Investing Networks and Communities:

Impact investing networks and communities provide valuable opportunities to connect with other impact investors, share best practices, and explore new investment opportunities. Here are five of the top impact investing networks and communities:

1. **Impact Hub:** Impact Hub is a global network of coworking spaces dedicated to promoting social and environmental impact. They provide various services, including networking events, workshops, and mentorship programs.
2. **Toniic:** Toniic is a global network of impact investors committed to using their capital to create positive social and environmental change. They provide various services, including education, networking, and investment opportunities.
3. **Social Venture Circle:** Social Venture Circle is a network of impact investors, social entrepreneurs, and other stakeholders committed to using business as a force for good. They provide various services, including networking events, mentorship programs, and investment opportunities.
4. **Investors' Circle:** Investors' Circle is a network of impact investors committed to using their capital to create positive social and environmental change. They provide various services, including networking events, mentorship programs, and investment opportunities.
5. **Confluence Philanthropy:** Confluence Philanthropy is a network of impact investors and philanthropists committed to using their capital to create positive social and environmental change. They provide various services, including networking events, educational programs, and investment opportunities.

Impact Investing Tools and Resources:

Impact investing tools and resources provide valuable insights and information to help investors make informed investment decisions and maximize their impact. Here are five of the top impact investing tools and resources:

1. **ImpactBase:** ImpactBase is a global database of impact investment funds, products, and services. It provides investors various tools and resources to help them identify and evaluate impact investment opportunities.
2. **IRIS:** IRIS is a set of standardized metrics used to measure impact investments' social, environmental, and financial performance. It provides investors a common language for measuring impact and comparing investment opportunities.
3. **GIIRS:** GIIRS is a rating system used to assess companies' and funds' social and environmental impact. It provides investors with a standardized way to evaluate the impact of their investments and compare investment opportunities.
4. **B Analytics:** B Analytics is a platform that provides companies with tools and resources to measure and improve their social and environmental impact. It also provides investors a way to evaluate the impact of their investments in certified B Corporations.
5. **Impact Investing Handbook:** The Impact Investing Handbook is a comprehensive guide to impact investing. It provides investors with practical tools and resources to help them make informed investment decisions and maximize their impact.

Impact investing is a powerful tool for creating positive social and environmental change while earning a financial return. Investors can make informed investment decisions and maximize their impact by leveraging the resources provided by impact investing organizations, publications, conferences, events, networks, communities, and tools. Whether you are a seasoned impact investor or just getting started, these resources can help you achieve your goals and make a difference in the world.

Chapter Summary

- Impact investing organizations provide research, education, networking, and investment opportunities.
- Impact investing publications provide insights and information about the field's latest trends, best practices, and success stories.
- Impact investing conferences and events provide valuable opportunities to network, learn, and explore new investment opportunities.
- Impact investing networks and communities provide valuable opportunities to connect with other impact investors, share best practices, and explore new investment opportunities.
- Impact investing tools and resources provide valuable insights and information to help investors make informed investment decisions and maximize their impact.
- The Global Impact Investing Network, ImpactAlpha, SOCAP, Impact Hub, and ImpactBase are among the top impact investing resources.
- IRIS, GIIRS, B Analytics, the Impact Investing Handbook, and the Skoll World Forum are among the top impact investing tools and resources.
- By leveraging these resources, investors can make informed investment decisions and maximize their impact.

EPILOGUE

As we come to the end of this book, it is important to reflect on the key takeaways and implications of impact investing. Impact investing is a powerful tool that combines financial returns with social and environmental impact. It can transform how we invest and create positive change in the world.

Summary of Impact Investing

Impact investing is a rapidly growing field that seeks to generate measurable social and environmental impact alongside financial returns. It is driven by a desire to address pressing global challenges such as poverty, inequality, climate change, and access to healthcare and education. Impact investors use various strategies and approaches to achieve their goals, including socially responsible investing, community investing, microfinance, and impact bonds.

Impact Investing and Social Change

Impact investing has the potential to create significant social change by directing capital toward businesses and organizations that are working to solve social and environmental problems. By investing in these organizations, impact investors can help to create jobs, improve access to essential services, and promote sustainable development. Impact investing can also shift the financial industry's focus towards more socially responsible and sustainable practices.

Impact Investing and the Future of the World

The world's future depends on our ability to address our complex social and environmental challenges. Impact investing can be critical in this effort by directing capital towards solutions that create positive social and environmental impact. In addition, by investing in businesses and organizations working to address these challenges, impact investors can help create a more sustainable and equitable future for all.

Impact Investing and You

Impact investing is not just for institutional investors or high-net-worth individuals. Anyone can become an impact investor by directing their investments towards businesses and organizations that align with their values and goals. Whether investing in a community development fund, supporting a social enterprise, or investing in renewable energy, your investments can make a difference.

Final Thoughts on Impact Investing

In conclusion, impact investing is a powerful tool that can help to create positive social and environmental impact while generating financial returns. It has the potential to transform the financial industry and create a more sustainable and equitable future for all. As you consider your investments, we encourage you to explore the world of impact investing and discover how you can make a difference.

ACKNOWLEDGMENTS

Writing a book is a journey; I could not have done it alone. So I want to express my deepest gratitude to the many people who have helped me along the way.

First and foremost, I would like to thank my family for their unwavering support and encouragement throughout the writing of this book. Their love and patience have been a constant source of inspiration; I could not have done this without them.

I also extend my deepest gratitude to my mentor Justina, whose guidance and wisdom have been invaluable in shaping my understanding of impact investing. Her insights and expertise have been instrumental in the development of this book.

I am also grateful to the team at Book Bound Studios for their support and guidance throughout the publishing process. The cover and interior design work provided by the team were amazing and exceeded my expectations.

I would also like to thank the many experts and practitioners in the field of impact investing who have shared their time and knowledge with me. Their insights and experiences have been invaluable in the development of this book.

Finally, thank you, the reader, for your interest in this topic. I hope this book will be a valuable resource for those looking to understand and implement impact strategies in their investment decisions.

Thank you all for your support and encouragement.

ABOUT THE AUTHOR

Robert Buckley is a financial professional with over 15 years of experience in the industry. He is a specialist in ESG and impact investing and has spent the past decade researching and studying the field. He has held various positions in the investment management sector, including portfolio management, research, and strategy development.

Robert is passionate about promoting sustainable and responsible investing and is dedicated to helping investors understand the benefits and risks of incorporating ESG factors in their investment decisions. He believes that by considering ESG factors, investors can achieve both financial returns and positively impact the world.

Robert enjoys hiking, reading, and spending time with his family in his free time.

$10.99 FREE EBOOK

Receive Your Free Copy of The Power of Intelligent Investing

Or visit:
bookboundstudios.wixsite.com/robert-buckley

Manufactured by Amazon.ca
Bolton, ON

40353927R00066